501 QUOTES ABOUT LOVE FUNNY, INSPIRATIONAL AND ROMANTIC QUOTES

M.PREFONTAINE

https://twitter.com/quotes4livingby

https://www.facebook.com/QuotesForLivingby/

INTRODUCTION

What is love? Surprisingly that is one of the most googled questions of all. The question then is do all these people not really know what love is? Why should they be interested what other people think about love?

Love is indeed a many splendored thing and is something that most people understand intuitively from their own experience. However it is difficult to capture those many feelings and thoughts in words. Perhaps it is difficult because love is not one thing but many things. There is love for your children, partner, parents, friends or even God are all different and each of these have their own multitude of variants.

Perhaps people are looking for confirmation of their own feelings in what others say to better understand them. It may be that they are looking to add zest to their own billet-doux or perhaps many just enjoy reading the thoughts and insights of others of something which is the essence of life.

Whatever your reason for reading this book I hope you enjoy my selection.

1.

A dream you dream alone is only a dream.
A dream you dream together is reality.

John Lennon

2.

To love is nothing. To be loved is
something. But to love and be loved, that's
everything.

T. Tolis

3.

Love begins with a smile, grows with a kiss,
and ends with a teardrop.

Augustine of Hippo

4.

All you need is love. But a little chocolate
now and then doesn't hurt.

Charles Schulz

5.

Three things I want in a relationship - Eyes
that won't cry, lips than won't lie, and love
that won't die.

Wiz Khalifa

6.

The sexiest thing a man can do for a
woman is crawl inside her mind and make
her imagination run wild

Anon

7.

Once in a while, right in the middle of an ordinary life, love gives us a fairy tale.

Anon

8.

To be happy with a man you must understand him a lot and love him a little. To be happy with a woman you must love her a lot and not try to understand her at all.

Helen Rowland

9.

Find a guy who calls you beautiful instead of hot, who calls you back when you hang up on him, who will lie under the stars and listen to your heartbeat, or will stay awake just to watch you sleep... wait for the boy who kisses your forehead, who wants to show you off to the world when you are in sweats, who holds your hand in front of his friends, who thinks you're just as pretty without makeup on. One who is constantly reminding you of how much he cares and how lucky his is to have you.... The one who turns to his friends and says, 'that's her.'

Chuck Palahniuk

10.

I have found the paradox, that if you love until it hurts, there can be no more hurt, only more love.

Mother Teresa

11.

Being deeply loved by someone gives you strength, while loving someone deeply gives you courage.

Lao Tzu

12.

What is Love? I have met in the streets a very poor young man who was in love. His hat was old, his coat worn, the water passed through his shoes and the stars through his soul.

Victor Hugo

13.

A man is already halfway in love with any woman who listens to him.

Brendan Francis

14.

We're born alone, we live alone, we die alone. Only through our love and friendship can we create the illusion for the moment that we're not alone.

Orson Welles

15.

As soon go kindle fire with snow, as seek to quench the fire of love with words.

William Shakespeare

16.

Love seems the swiftest, but it is the slowest of all growths. No man or woman really knows what perfect love is until they have been married a quarter of a century.

Mark Twain

17.

A pair of powerful spectacles has sometimes sufficed to cure a person in love.

Friedrich Nietzsche

18.

Sacrificing your happiness for the happiness of the one you love, is by far, the truest type of love.

Henry David Thoreau

19.

Love yourself first and everything else falls into line. You really have to love yourself to get anything done in this world.

Lucille Ball

20.

Life is the flower for which love is the honey.

Victor Hugo

21.

Love is the delusion that one woman differs from another.

H. L. Mencken

22.

If you wish to be loved, show more of your
faults than your virtues.

Edward G. Bulwer-Lytton

23.

Love isn't something you find. Love is
something that finds you.

Loretta Young

24.

How absurd and delicious it is to be in love
with somebody younger than yourself.
Everybody should try it.

Barbara Pym

25.

For small creatures such as we the vastness
is bearable only through love.

Carl Sagan

26.

Love is when you shed a tear and still want
him, it's when he ignores you and you still
love him, it's when he loves another girl
but you still smile and say I'm happy for
you, when all you really do is cry.

Anon

27.

It's useless to hold a person to anything he
says while he's in love, drunk, or running
for office.

Shirley MacLaine

28.

To love oneself is the beginning of a lifelong romance.

Oscar Wilde

29.

A moment in life - followed by an eternity of situations to grow from or regret - is the reality that love is not about winning or losing, but simply to survive.

William E Lewis

30.

People will forget what you said. People will forget what you did. But people will never forget how you made them feel.

Maya Angelou

31.

Love is like swallowing hot chocolate before it has cooled off. It takes you by surprise at first, but keeps you warm for a long time.

Henri Frederic Amiel

32.

I don't understand why Cupid was chosen to represent Valentine's Day. When I think about romance, the last thing on my mind is a short, chubby toddler coming at me with a weapon

Anon

33.
Learn to love without any conditions, help without any expectations and to live without any regrets.
Anurag Prakash Ray

34.
Love withers with predictability; its very essence is surprise and amazement. To make love a prisoner of the mundane is to take its passion and lose it forever.
Leo Buscaglia

35.
What the heart gives away is never gone ... It is kept in the hearts of others.
Robin St. John

36.
Time is too slow for those who wait, too swift for those who fear, too long for those who grieve, too short for those who rejoice, but for those who love, time is eternity.
Henry Van Dyke

37.
I love thee to the depth and breadth and height my soul can reach.
Elizabeth Barrett Browning

38.
Love is happiness given back and forth.
Anon

39.

Love built on beauty, soon as beauty, dies.

John Donne

40.

To love another person is to see the face of God.

Les Miserables

41.

A very small degree of hope is sufficient to cause the birth of love.

Stendhal

42.

In vain have I struggled. It will not do. My feelings will not be repressed. You must allow me to tell you how ardently I admire and love you.

Jane Austen, Pride And Prejudice

43.

Every love story is a tragedy, in the end, but that's what makes them so beautiful, so cherished in the minds and hearts of those who remember them.

D. Michael Hardy

44.

A friend is someone who knows all about you and still loves you.

Elbert Hubbard

45.

Don't come crawlin' to a man for love - he
likes to get a run for his money.

Mae West

46.

Have you ever been in love? Horrible isn't
it? It makes you so vulnerable. It opens
your chest and it opens up your heart and
it means that someone can get inside you
and mess you up.

Neil Gaiman

47.

I see when men love women they give but a
little of their lives, but women, when they
love, give everything.

Oscar Wilde

48.

I am nothing special, of this I am sure. I am
a common man with common thoughts and
I've led a common life. There are no
monuments dedicated to me and my name
will soon be forgotten, but I've loved
another with all my heart and soul, and to
me, this has always been enough.

Nicholas Sparks

49.

People think a soul mate is your perfect fit, and thats what everyone wants. But a true soul mate is a mirror, the person who shows you everything that is holding you back, the person who brings you to your own attention so you can change your life.

Anon

50.

In the arithmetic of love, one plus one equals everything, and two minus one equals nothing.

Mignon McLaughlin

51.

Love comes unseen; we only see it go.

Austin Dobson

52.

I no longer believed in the idea of soul mates, or love at first sight. But I was beginning to believe that a very few times in your life, if you were lucky, you might meet someone who was exactly right for you. Not because he was perfect, or because you were, but because your combined flaws were arranged in a way that allowed two separate beings to hinge together.

Lisa Kleypas

53.

Sometimes the smallest act of love can take up the biggest space in someone's heart.

Anon

54.

People love others not for who they are but for how they make them feel.

Irwin Federman

55.

So, I love you because the entire universe conspired to help me find you.

Paulo Coelho

56.

Some women choose to follow men, and some women choose to follow their dreams. If you're wondering which way to go, remember that your career will never wake up and tell you that it doesn't love you anymore.

Lady Gaga

57.

When you trip over love, it is easy to get up. But when you fall in love, it is impossible to stand again.

Anon

58.

There is always some madness in love. But there is also always some reason in madness.

Friedrich Nietzsche

59.

Any man who can drive safely while kissing a pretty girl is simply not giving the kiss the attention it deserves.

Albert Einstein

60.

Love is what makes two people sit in the middle of a bench when there is plenty of room at both ends.

Barbara Johnson

61.

I am not sure exactly what heaven will be like, but I know that when we die and it comes time for God to judge us, he will not ask, 'How many good things have you done in your life?' rather he will ask, 'How much love did you put into what you did?

Mother Teresa

62.

If you love something let it go free. If it doesn't come back, you never had it. If it comes back, love it forever.

Doug Horton

63.

Man may have discovered fire, but women discovered how to play with it.

Candace Bushnell

64.

**Meeting you was fate, becoming your
friend was a choice, but falling in love with
you I had no control over.**

Anon

65.

**The perfect love affair is one which is
conducted entirely by post.**

George Bernard Shaw

66.

**Pleasure of love lasts but a moment, Pain of
love lasts a lifetime.**

Bette Davis

67.

**Perhaps love is the process of my leading
you gently back to yourself**

Antoine de Saint-Exupery

68.

True Love burns the brightest, but the brightest flames leave the deepest scars. It is almost impossible to fall out of love, because once love's fire is able to burn inside of you, it becomes a part of you. No matter what we may feel or think we believe about a person who presently has your heart, chances are if you were in true love with someone before, a small piece of you will always be with them. The heart that has truly loved never forgets, it just continues to paddle forward in the stream of new love, hoping to eventually meet up with its true love once again.

Brandi Snyder

69.

Love is a deep well from which you may drink often, but into which you may fall but once.

Ellye Howell Glover

70.

Love is the exchange of two fantasies and the contact of two skins.

Nicolas Chamfort

71.

All love is unrequited. All of it.

J. Michael Straczynski

72.

To be kind to all, to like many and love a few, to be needed and wanted by those we love, is certainly the nearest we can come to happiness.

Mary Stuart

73.

Love is something far more than desire for sexual intercourse; it is the principal means of escape from the loneliness which afflicts most men and women throughout the greater part of their lives.

Bertrand Russell

74.

Love is a state in which a man sees things most decidedly as they are not.

Friedrich Nietzsche

75.

Fear less, hope more; Eat less, chew more; Whine less, breathe more; Talk less, say more; Love more, and all good things will be yours

Swedish Proverb

76.

If I never met you, I wouldn't like you. If I didn't like you, I wouldn't love you. If I didn't love you, I wouldn't miss you. But I did, I do, and I will.

Anon

77.

There's no love greater than mothers love, and there's no greater sacrifice than what a father does for his kids.

Anurag Prakash Ray

78.

Tell yourself you love yourself, even if you don't believe it, because this is when you really need to hear yourself say it.

Anon

79.

Until you get comfortable with being alone, you'll never know if you're choosing someone out of love or loneliness.

Anon

80.

They say a person needs just three things to be truly happy in this world: someone to love, something to do, and something to hope for.

Tom Bodett

81.

The love that lasts the longest is the love that is never returned.

William Somerset Maugham

82.

Darkness cannot drive out darkness: only light can do that. Hate cannot drive out hate: only love can do that.

Martin Luther King Jr

83.

Love looks not with the eyes, but with the mind,
And therefore is winged Cupid painted blind.

William Shakespeare

84.

You don't love someone because they're perfect, you love them in spite of the fact that they're not.

Jodi Picoult

85.

The real lover is the man who can thrill you by kissing your forehead or smiling into your eyes or just staring into space.

Marilyn Monroe

86.

The heart wants what it wants. There's no logic to these things. You meet someone and you fall in love and that's that.

Woody Allen

87.

I know they say that first love is the sweetest, but that first cut is the deepest.

Drake

88.

A kiss is a lovely trick designed by nature to stop speech when words become superfluous.

Ingrid Bergman

89.

When love is not madness, it is not love.

Pedro Calderon de la Barca

90.

Do I love you because you're beautiful, or are you beautiful because I love you?

Richard Rodgers and Oscar Hammerstein II, Cinderella

91.

Love is a two-way street constantly under construction.

Carroll Bryant

92.

Without love, what are we worth? Eighty-nine cents! Eighty-nine cents worth of chemicals walking around lonely.

Laurence Marks

93.

A man reserves his true and deepest love not for the species of woman in whose company he finds himself electrified and enkindled, but for that one in whose company he may feel tenderly drowsy.

George Jean Nathan

94.

A successful marriage requires falling in love many times, always with the same person.

Mignon McLaughlin

95.

Let there be spaces in your togetherness, and let the winds of the heavens dance between you. Love one another but make not a bond of love: Let it be rather a moving sea between the shores of your souls.

Kahlil Gibran

96.

There is no more lovely, friendly, and charming relationship, communion or company than a good marriage.

Martin Luther

97.

Falling in love is when she falls asleep in your arms and wakes up in your dreams.

Unknown

98.

Love is a smoke and is made with the fume of sighs.

William Shakespeare

99.

Love is composed of a single soul inhabiting two bodies.

Aristotle

100.
Seven days without love makes one weak.
Drake

101.
It is not a lack of love, but a lack of
friendship that makes unhappy marriages.
Friedrich Nietzsche

102.
The best and most beautiful things in this
world cannot be seen or even heard, but
must be felt with the heart.
Helen Keller

103.
Love is like war: easy to begin but very
hard to stop.
H. L. Mencken

104.
Love is so short, forgetting is so long.
Pablo Neruda

105.
You know its love when all you want is that
person to be happy, even if you're not part
of their happiness.
Julia Roberts

106.
A lady's imagination is very rapid; it jumps
from admiration to love, from love to
matrimony in a moment.
Jane Austen

107.
Tis better to have loved and lost
Than never to have loved at all.
Alfred Lord Tennyson

108.
When two people love each other, they
don't look at each other, they look in the
same direction.
Ginger Rogers

109.
There is no surprise more magical than the
surprise of being loved. It is God's finger on
man's shoulder. *Charles Morgan*

110.
And in the end, the love you take, is equal
to the love you make.
Paul McCartney

111.
Love is the only sane and satisfactory
answer to the problem of human existence.
Erich Fromm

112.
Let your love be like the misty rains,
coming softly, but flooding the river.
Madagascar Proverb

113.

A guy and a girl can be just friends, but at one point or another, they will fall for each other...Maybe temporarily, maybe at the wrong time, maybe too late, or maybe forever

Dave Matthews Band

114.

Love one another and you will be happy. It's as simple and as difficult as that.

Michael Leunig

115.

Love at first sight is easy to understand; it's when two people have been looking at each other for a lifetime that it becomes a miracle.

Sam Levenson

116.

He that falls in love with himself will have no rivals.

Benjamin Franklin

117.

A wise girl kisses but doesn't love, listens but doesn't believe, and leaves before she is left.

Marilyn Monroe

118.

When you look for the right person, you always end up with the wrong one. But when you just sit by the corner and wait, he comes along and shares the corner with you.

Anon

119.

You don't love someone for their looks, or their clothes, or for their fancy car, but because they sing a song only you can hear.

Oscar Wilde

120.

Two souls with but a single thought; two hearts that beat as one.

Friedrich Halm

121.

A flower cannot blossom without sunshine, and man cannot live without love

Max Muller

122.

Affection is responsible for nine-tenths of whatever solid and durable happiness there is in our lives.

C. S. Lewis

123.

If two past lovers can remain friends, its either they are still in love, or never were.

Anon

124.

For it was not into my ear you whispered,
but into my heart. It was not my lips you
kissed, but my soul.

Judy Garland

125.

Let us always meet each other with smile,
for the smile is the beginning of love.

Mother Teresa

126

Break a vase, and the love that reassembles
the fragments is stronger than that love
which took its symmetry for granted when
it was whole.

Derek Walcott

127.

Absence diminishes mediocre passions and
increases great ones, as the wind
extinguishes candles and fans fires.

Francois de La Rochefoucauld

128.

If you love two people at the same time,
choose the second one, because if you
really loved the first one you wouldn't have
fallen for the second.

Johnny Depp

129.

Come live in my heart, and pay no rent.

Samuel Lover

130.
All love shifts and changes. I don't know if you can be wholeheartedly in love all the time.
Julie Andrews

131.
Love is that condition in which the happiness of another person is essential to your own.
Robert A. Heinlein

132.
We are most alive when we're in love.
John Updike

133.
Love means never having to say you're sorry.
Ali MacGraw

134.
One word frees us of all the weight and pain of life: That word is love.
Sophocles

135.
You are my best friend as well as my lover, and I do not know which side of you I enjoy the most. I treasure each side, just as I have treasured our life together.
Nicholas Sparks

136.
Where there is love there is life.
Mahatma Gandhi

137.
Love has no desire but to fulfill itself. To melt and be like a running brook that sings its melody to the night. To wake at dawn with a winged heart and give thanks for another day of loving.
Khalil Gibran

138.
Love is a symbol of eternity. It wipes out all sense of time, destroying all memory of a beginning and all fear of an end.
Anon

139.
Love is an act of endless forgiveness, a tender look which becomes a habit.
Peter Ustinov

140.
Who would give a law to lovers? Love is unto itself a higher law.
Boethius

141.
The art of love... is largely the art of persistence.
Albert Ellis

142.

Love — a wildly misunderstood although highly desirable malfunction of the heart which weakens the brain, causes eyes to sparkle, cheeks to glow, blood pressure to rise and the lips to pucker.

Anon

143.

What greater thing is there for two human souls, than to feel that they are joined for life–to strength each other in all labor, to rest on each other in all sorrow, to minister to each other in silent unspeakable memories at the moment of the last parting

George Eliot

144.

A happy marriage is a long conversation which always seems too short.

Andre Marois

145.

When I saw you I fell in love, and you smiled because you knew.

Arrigo Boito

146.

Sexiness is a state of mind - a comfortable state of being. It's about loving yourself in your most unlovable moments.

Halle Berry

147.

Love is the voice under all silences, the hope which has no opposite in fear; the strength so strong mere force is feebleness: the truth more first than sun, more last than star.

e.e. cummings

148.

It takes a minute to have a crush on someone, an hour to like someone and a day to love someone - but it takes a lifetime to forget someone.

Johnny Depp

149.

Walking with your hands in mine and mine in yours, that's exactly where I want to be always.

Fawn Weaver

150.

Woe to the man whose heart has not learned while young to hope, to love – and to put its trust in life.

Joseph Conrad

151.

Smart girls open their mind, easy girls open their legs, and foolish girls open their heart.

Anon

152.

Keep love in your heart. A life without it is like a sunless garden when the flowers are dead.

Oscar Wilde

153.

Friends can help each other. A true friend is someone who lets you have total freedom to be yourself - and especially to feel. Or, not feel. Whatever you happen to be feeling at the moment is fine with them. That's what real love amounts to - letting a person be what he really is.

Jim Morrison

154.

You can close your eyes to the things you do not want to see, but you cannot close your heart to the things you do not want to feel.

Johnny Depp

155.

I love everybody. Some I love to be around, some I love to avoid, and others I would love to punch in the face!

Senora Roy

156.

Being single does not mean no one wants you...it just means that God is busy writing your love story.

Anon

157.

Its beauty that captures your attention;
personality which captures your heart.

Oscar Wilde

158.

If you press me to say why I loved him, I
can say no more than because he was he,
and I was I.

Michel de Montaigne

159.

Everyone says that love hurts. But that's
not true. Loneliness hurts, rejection hurts,
losing someone hurts. Everyone confuses
these with love, but in reality love is the
only thing in this world that covers up all
the pain and makes us feel wonderful
again.

Meša Selimović

160.

Love is always bestowed as a gift - freely,
willingly and without expectation. We
don't love to be loved; we love to love.

Leo Buscaglia

161.
I believe that imagination is stronger than knowledge. That myth is more potent than history. That dreams are more powerful than facts. That hope always triumphs over experience. That laughter is the only cure for grief. And I believe that love is stronger than death.
Robert Fulghum

162.
With love one can live even without happiness.
Fyodor Dostoyevsky

163.
In order to be happy oneself it is necessary to make at least one other person happy.
Theodor Reik

164.
If I know what love is, it is because of you.
Herman Hesse

165.
People must learn to hate and if they can learn to hate, they can be taught to love.
Nelson Mandela

166.
We are shaped and fashioned by those we love.
Geothe

167.

Before I met my husband, I'd never fallen
in love. I'd stepped in it a few times.

Rita Rudner

168.

You know you're in love when you can't fall
asleep because reality is finally better than
your dreams.

Dr. Seuss

169.

There is never a time or place for true love.
It happens accidentally, in a heartbeat, in a
single flashing, throbbing moment.

Sarah Dessen,

170.

Just when you think it can't get any worse,
it can. And just when you think it can't get
any better, it can.

Nicholas Sparks

171.

Sex is like money; only too much is enough.

John Updike

172.

Always remember you are braver than you
believe, stronger than you seem, smarter
than you think and twice as beautiful as
you've ever imagined.

Dr. Seuss

173.

Love recognizes no barriers. It jumps hurdles, leaps fences, penetrates walls to arrive at its destination full of hope.

Maya Angelou

174.

Love is like the wind, you can't see it but you can feel it.

Nicholas Sparks

175.

What greater thing is there for two human souls, than to feel that they are joined for life–to strength each other in all labor, to rest on each other in all sorrow, to minister to each other in silent unspeakable memories at the moment of the last parting?

George Eliot

176.

A woman knows the face of the man she loves as a sailor knows the open sea.

Honore de Balzac

177.

Who, being loved, is poor?

Oscar Wilde

178.

When marrying, ask yourself this question: Do you believe that you will be able to converse well with this person into your old age? Everything else in marriage is transitory.

Friedrich Nietzsche

179.

The heart has its reasons which reason knows not.

Blaise Pascal

180.

Nothing takes the taste out of peanut butter quite like unrequited love.

Charles M. Schulz

181.

Romance is the glamor which turns the dust of everyday life into a golden haze.

Elinor Glyn

182.

Out beyond ideas of wrongdoing and rightdoing there is a field. I'll meet you there. When the soul lies down in that grass the world is too full to talk about.

Rumi

183.

When you love someone, all your saved-up wishes start coming out.

Elizabeth Bowen

184.

To love and be loved is to feel the sun from both sides.

David Viscott

185.

Love those who love you.

Voltaire

186.

Think not because you are now wed, that all your courtship's at an end.

Antonio Hurtado de Mendoza

187.

Just because someone doesn't love you in the way you want them to, doesn't mean that they don't love you with all they've got.

Anon

188.

Happiness is anyone and anything at all, that's loved by you.

Charlie Brown

189.

I love being married. It's so great to find that one special person you want to annoy for the rest of your life.

Rita Rudner

190.

Love must be as much a light, as it is a flame.

Henry David Thoreau

191.

The truth is everyone is going to hurt you.
You just got to find the ones worth
suffering for.
Bob Marley

192.

If you love a flower, don't pick it up.
Because if you pick it up, it dies and it
ceases to be what you love. So if you love a
flower, let it be. Love is not about
possession. It is about appreciation.
Osho

193.

Love is a friendship set to music.
Joseph Campbell

194.

Some love stories aren't epic novels. Some
are short stories, but that doesn't make
them any less filled with love.
Carrie Bradshaw

195.

The strongest love is the love that can
demonstrate its fragility.
Paulo Coelho

196.

True love stories never have endings.
Richard Bach

197.
There is no disguise which can hide love for long where it exists, or simulate it where it does not.

La Rochefoucauld

198.
Blushing is the color of virtue.

Diogenes

199.
There is no remedy for love but to love more.

Henry David Thoreau

200.
The best things in life are never rationed. Friendship, royalty and love do not require coupons.

George T Hewitt

201.
The only creatures that are evolved enough to convey pure love are dogs and infants

Johnny Depp

202.
People fall in love without reason, without even wanting to. You can't predict it. That's love.

Haruki Murakami

203.

I'm selfish, impatient and a little insecure. I make mistakes, I am out of control and at times hard to handle. But if you can't handle me at my worst, then you sure as hell don't deserve me at my best.

Marilyn Monroe

204.

Unless you love someone, nothing else makes any sense.

e.e. Cummings

205.

The greatest thing you'll ever learn is just to love and be loved in return.

eden ahbez

206.

Time has no dominion over love. Love is the one thing that transcends time.

Jeaniene Frost

207.

It is love alone that gives worth to all things.

Teresa of Ávila

208.

Love weaves itself from hundreds of threads.

David Levithan

209.
A rose without thorns is like love without heartbreak; it doesn't make sense.
Anatole France

210.
To fall in love is to create a religion that has a fallible god.
Jorge Luis Borges

211.
Life's a game made for everyone, and love is the prize.
Tim Bergling

212.
Love is trembling happiness.
Khalil Gibron

213.
Without love we are like birds with broken wings.
Mitch Albom

214.
Love me like you'll never see me again.
Alicia Keys

215.
Love is like pi - natural, irrational, and very important.
Lisa Hoffman

216.
We come to love not by finding a perfect person, but by learning to see an imperfect person perfectly.
Sam Keen

217.
In true love the smallest distance is too great, and the greatest distance can be bridged.
Hans Nouwens

218.
Love is the only force capable of transforming an enemy to a friend.
Martin Luther King Jr.

219.
We love the things we love for what they are.
Robert Frost

220.
Most people have a harder time letting themselves love than finding someone to love them.
Bill Russell

221.
Love me when I least deserve it, because that's when I really need it.
Swedish proverb

222.
The greater your capacity to love, the greater your capacity to feel the pain.
Jennifer Anniston

223.
I heard what you said. I'm not the silly romantic you think. I don't want the heavens or the shooting stars. I don't want gemstones or gold. I have those things already. I want...a steady hand. A kind soul. I want to fall asleep, and wake, knowing my heart is safe. I want to love, and be loved.
Shana Abe

224.
Love is the magician that pulls man out of his own hat.
Ben Hecht

225.
We love because it's the only true adventure.
Nikki Giovanni

226.
Ah me! love can not be cured by herbs.
Ovid

227.
Love has nothing to do with what you are expecting to get — only with what you are expecting to give — which is everything.
Maria Popova

228.
Love is only a dirty trick played on us to
achieve continuation of the species.
W. Somerset Maugham

229.
Never love anyone who treats you like
you're ordinary.
Oscar Wilde

230.
Forget love — I'd rather fall in chocolate!
Sandra J. Dykes

231
Love is a sweet tyranny, because the lover
endureth his torments willingly.
Proverb

232
Hate leaves ugly scars, love leaves
beautiful ones.
Mignon McLaughlin

233.
To love someone is nothing, to be loved by
someone is something, but to be loved by
the one you love is everything.
Bill Russell

234.
To find someone who will love you for no
reason, and to shower that person with
reasons, that is the ultimate happiness.
Robert Brault

235.

He's more myself than I am. Whatever our souls are made of, his and mine are the same.

Emily Brontë

236.

A baby is born with a need to be loved — and never outgrows it.

Frank A. Clark

237.

Love doesn't just sit there, like a stone, it has to be made, like bread; remade all the time, made new.

Ursula K. Le Guin

238.

Love is, above all, the gift of oneself.

Jean Anouilh

239.

When a man is in love or in debt, someone else has the advantage.

Bill Balance

240.

Anyone can be passionate, but it takes real lovers to be silly.

Rose Franken

241.

In dreams and in love there are no impossibilities.

Janos Arnay

242.

Love is like dew that falls on both nettles and lilies.

Swedish Proverb

243.

Since love grows within you, so beauty grows. For love is the beauty of the soul.

Saint Augustine

244.

Passion makes the world go round. Love just makes it a safer place.

Ice T

245.

Love is an ocean of emotions entirely surrounded by expenses. *Lord Dewar*

246.

You know you have found love when you can't find your way back.

Robert Brault

247.

Love is an exploding cigar we willingly smoke.

Lynda Barry

248.

Love is all fun and games until someone loses an eye or gets pregnant.

Jim Cole

249.

Love is the ultimate outlaw. It just won't adhere to any rules. The most any of us can do is sign on as its accomplice.

Tom Watson

250.

Love is saying 'I feel differently' instead of 'You're wrong.'

Brandi Snyder

251.

Sometimes the heart sees what is invisible to the eye.

H. Jackson Brown, Jr.

252.

Love does not dominate; it cultivates.

Johann Wolfgang von Goethe

253.

A loving heart is the beginning of all knowledge.

Thomas Carlyle

254

A kiss makes the heart young again and wipes out the years.

Rupert Brooke

255.

At the touch of love everyone becomes a poet.

Plato

256

I was born with an enormous need for
affection, and a terrible need to give it.

Audrey Hepburn

257.

Love is a force more formidable than any
other. It is invisible - it cannot be seen or
measured, yet it is powerful enough to
transform you in a moment, and offer you
more joy than any material possession
could.

Barbara de Angelis

258.

A loving heart is the truest wisdom.

Charles Dickens

259.

Faith makes all things possible.
love makes all things easy.

Dwight L. Moody

260.

The best thing to hold onto in life is each
other.

Audrey Hepburn

261.

Love is life. And if you miss love, you miss
life.

Leo Buscaglia

262.
First love is only a little foolishness and a lot of curiosity.
George Bernard Shaw

263.
I was about half in love with her by the time we sat down. That's the thing about girls. Every time they do something pretty... you fall half in love with them, and then you never know where the hell you are.
J. D. Salinger

264.
Love is the flower you've got to let grow
John Lennon

265.
If you want to be loved, be lovable.
Ovid

266.
Hatred paralyzes life; love releases it. Hatred confuses life; love harmonizes it. Hatred darkens life; love illuminates it.
Martin Luther King Jr.

267.
Love can sometimes be magic. But magic can sometimes... just be an illusion.
Javan

268.

To fear love is to fear life, and those who fear life are already three parts dead.

Bertrand Russell

269.

All mankind love a lover.

Ralph Waldo Emerson

270.

The one thing we can never get enough of is love. And the one thing we never give enough is love.

Henry Miller

271.

Love is the beauty of the soul.

Saint Augustine

272.

Absence - that common cure of love.

Lord Byron

273.

Love is an irresistible desire to be irresistibly desired.

Robert Frost

274.

Everything is clearer when you're in love.

John Lennon

275.

The moment you have in your heart this extraordinary thing called love and feel the depth, the delight, the ecstasy of it, you will discover that for you the world is transformed.

Jiddu Krishnamurti

276.

Love is a game that two can play and both win.

Eva Gabor

277.

It is difficult to know at what moment love begins; it is less difficult to know that it has begun.

Henry Wadsworth Longfellow

278.

You will find as you look back upon your life that the moments when you have truly lived are the moments when you have done things in the spirit of love.

Henry Drummond

279.

The hours I spend with you I look upon as sort of a perfumed garden, a dim twilight, and a fountain singing to it. You and you alone make me feel that I am alive. Other men it is said have seen angels, but I have seen thee and thou art enough.

George Edward Moore

280.
Looking back, I have this to regret, that too often when I loved, I did not say so

David Grayson

281.
I believe in the compelling power of love. I do not understand it. I believe it to be the most fragrant blossom of all this thorny existence.

Theodore Dreiser

282.
Life without love is like a tree without blossoms or fruit.

Khalil Gibran

283.
Fortune and love favor the brave.

Ovid

284.
The best proof of love is trust.

Joyce Brothers

285.
Love consists in this, that two solitudes protect and touch and greet each other.

Rainer Maria Rilke

286.
What we have once enjoyed we can never lose. All that we love deeply becomes a part of us.

Helen Keller

287.

He felt now that he was not simply close to her, but that he did not know where he ended and she began.

Leo Tolstoy

288.

A soulmate is the one person whose love is powerful enough to motivate you to meet your soul, to do the emotional work of self-discovery, of awakening.

Kenny Loggins

289.

True love begins when nothing is looked for in return.

Antoine De Saint-Exupery

290.

Love is the emblem of eternity: it confounds all notion of time: effaces all memory of a beginning, all fear of an end.

Germaine De Stael

291.

Love is not a matter of counting the years...But making the years count.

Michelle St. Amand

292.

Love is a beautiful red rose given for no apparent reason.

Anon

293.

Love is like a river, never ending as it flows, but gets greater with time!

Anon

294.

True love is eternal, infinite, and always like itself. It is equal and pure, without violent demonstrations: it is seen with white hairs and is always young in the heart.

Honore de Balzac

295.

A mighty pain to love it is, and 'tis a pain that pain to miss; but of all the pains, the greatest pain is to love, but love in vain.

Abraham Crowley

296.

You don't marry someone you can live with – you marry the person who you cannot live without.

Anon

297.

I never knew how to worship until I knew how to love.

Henry Ward Beecher

298.

Love is blind, but friendship closes its eyes.

Anon

299.

True love is like ghosts, which everybody
talks about and few have seen.

La Rochefoucauld

300.

Whoever loved that loved not at first sight?

Christopher Marlowe

301.

We perceive when love begins and when it
declines by our embarrassment when
alone together.

La Bruyere

302.

Life has taught us that love does not consist
in gazing at each other but in looking
outward together in the same direction.

Saint-Exupery

303.

Love is but the discovery of ourselves in
others, and the delight in the recognition.

Alexander Smith

304.

Tell me whom you love and I will tell you
who you are.

Houssaye

305.

Sympathy constitutes friendship; but in love there is a sort of antipathy, or opposing passion. Each strives to be the other, and both together make up one whole.

Samuel Taylor Coleridge

306.

When we are in love we often doubt that which we most believe.

La Rochefoucauld

307.

The richest love is that which submits to the arbitration of time.

Lawrence Durrell

308.

Death is a challenge. It tells us not to waste time... It tells us to tell each other right now that we love each other

Leo F. Buscaglia

309.

Love cures people – both the ones who give it and the ones who receive it.

Dr. Karl Menninger

310.

Friendship often ends in love; but love in friendship – never.

Charles Caleb Colton

311.

Falling in love consists merely in uncorking the imagination and bottling the common sense.

Helen Rowland

312.

Somewhere there is someone that dreams of your smile, and finds in your presence that life is worthwhile, so when you are lonely remember its true, someone somewhere is thinking of you.

Atul Purohit

313.

A woman has got to love a bad man once or twice in her life, to be thankful for a good one.

Marjorie Kinnan Rawlings

314.

The big difference between sex for money and sex for free is that sex for money usually costs a lot less.

Brendan Behan

315.

Loving can cost a lot but not loving always costs more, and those who fear to love often find that want of love is an emptiness that robs the joy from life.

Merle Shain

316.

We accept the love we think we deserve.

Stephen Chbosky

317.

It is better to be hated for what you are
than to be loved for what you are not.

André Gide

318.

I can live without money, but I cannot live
without love.

Judy Garland

319.

Love is the flower of life, and blossoms
unexpectedly and without law, and must be
plucked where it is found, and enjoyed for
the brief hour of its duration.

DH Lawrence

320.

Many men kill themselves for love, but
many more women die of it.

Helen Rowland

321.

In love, women are professionals, men are
amateurs.

Francois Truffaut

322.

If you can make a woman laugh, you can
make her do anything.

Marilyn Monroe

323.
Love never dies a natural death. It dies because we don't know how to replenish its source. It dies of blindness and errors and betrayals. It dies of illness and wounds; it dies of weariness, of witherings, of tarnishings.
Anaïs Nin

324.
If I had a flower for every time I thought of you...I could walk through my garden forever.
Alfred Lord Tennyson

325.
Love wasn't put in your heart to stay. Love isn't love until you give it away.
Michael W. Smith

326.
Real love is more than a physical feeling. If there's even the slightest doubt in your head about a guy, then forget about it. It's not real.
Ethan Embry

326.
You have to walk carefully in the beginning of love; the running across fields into your lover's arms can only come later when you're sure they won't laugh if you trip.
Jonathan Carroll

327.
Love is the condition in which the
happiness of another person is essential to
your own.
Robert Heinlein

328.
This is a good sign, having a broken heart.
It means we have tried for something.
Elizabeth Gilbert

329.
The more I know of the world, the more I
am convinced that I shall never see a man
whom I can really love. I require so much!
Jane Austen

330.
I don't want to live. I want to love first, and
live incidentally.
Zelda Fitzgerald

331.
We waste time looking for the perfect
lover, instead of creating the perfect love.
Tom Robbins

332.
Pure love produces pure nonsense.
Jonathan Klinger

333.

When a love comes to an end, weaklings cry, efficient ones instantly find another love, and the wise already have one in reserve.

Oscar Wilde

334.

Two people in love, alone, isolated from the world, that's beautiful.

Milan Kundera

335.

Love is a fire. But whether it is going to warm your hearth or burn down your house, you can never tell.

Joan Crawford

336.

He's more myself than I am. Whatever our souls are made of, his and mine are the same.

Emily Brontë

337.

I love you not because of who you are, but because of who I am when I am with you.

Roy Croft

338.

For the two of us, home isn't a place. It is a person. And we are finally home.

Stephanie Perkins

339.

The very essence of romance is
uncertainty.

Oscar Wilde

340.

Hatred is blind, as well as love.

Oscar Wilde

341.

Love does not begin and end the way we
seem to think it does. Love is a battle, love
is a war; love is a growing up.

James Baldwin

342.

People who are sensible about love are
incapable of it.

Douglas Yates

343.

One of the hardest things in life is watching
the person you love, love someone else.

Anon

344.

I have decided to stick to love...Hate is too
great a burden to bear.

Martin Luther King Jr

345.

If you have to think about whether you love
someone or not then the answer is no.
When you love someone you just know.

Janice Markowitz

346.

When one is in love, one always begins by deceiving one's self, and one always ends by deceiving others. That is what world calls a romance.

Oscar Wilde

347.

The more I give to thee, the more I have, for both are infinite.

William Shakespeare

348.

Love is like an hourglass, with the heart filling up as the brain empties.

Jules Renard

349.

The beginning of love is to let those we love be perfectly themselves, and not to twist them to fit our own image. Otherwise we love only the reflection of ourselves we find in them.

Thomas Merton

350.

Love is much like a wild rose, beautiful and calm, but willing to draw blood in its defense.

Mark Overby

351.

Eventually you will come to understand that love heals everything, and love is all there is.

Gary Zukav

352.
Love is being stupid together.
Paul Valery

353.
Love is not written on paper, for paper can be erased. Nor is it etched on stone, for stone can be broken. But it is inscribed on a heart and there it shall remain forever.
Jalal Ad-Din Rumi

354.
Love is of all passions the strongest, for it attacks simultaneously the head, the heart and the senses.
Lao Tzu

355.
The quickest way to receive love is to give; the fastest way to lose love is to hold it too tightly; and the best way to keep love is to give it wings.
Bill Russell

356.
Love is more afraid of change than destruction.
Friedrich Nietzsche

357.
The greatest pain that comes from love is loving someone you can never have.
Anon

358.
They are wrong who say that love is blind.
On the contrary, nothing - not even the
smallest detail - escapes the eyes; one sees
everything in the loved one, notices
everything; but melts it all into one flame
with the great and simple: I love you.
Gregory J P Godek

359.
Life without love is a shadow of things that
might be.
Neil Galman

360.
The difference between friendship and
love is how much you can hurt each other.
Ashleigh Brilliant

361.
Love is the Fire of Life; it either consumes
or purifies.
Swedish Proverb

362.
Love is a lot like dancing-you just
surrender to the music.
Mary Oliver

363.
The opposite of love is not hate, its
indifference.
Elie Wiesel

364.

To love at all is to be vulnerable. Love
anything, and your heart will certainly be
wrung and possibly broken. If you want to
make sure of keeping it intact, you must
give your heart to no one, not even to an
animal. Wrap it carefully round with
hobbies and little luxuries; avoid all
entanglements; lock it up safe in the casket
or coffin of your selfishness. But in that
casket- safe, dark, motionless, airless--it
will change. It will not be broken; it will
become unbreakable, impenetrable,
irredeemable.

C.S. Lewis

365.

Love is born with the pleasure of looking at
each other, it is fed with the necessity of
seeing each other, it is concluded with the
impossibility of separation.

Mark Overby

366.

Love is never wrong.

Melissa Etheridge

367.

Love is the harmony of two souls singing
together.

Gregory J. P. Godek

368.

Love is like an earthquake-unpredictable, a little scary, but when the hard part is over you realize how lucky you truly are.

James Earl Jones

369.

Love is like a friendship caught on fire. In the beginning a flame, very pretty, often hot and fierce, but still only light and flickering. As love grows older, our hearts mature and our love becomes as coals, deep-burning and unquenchable.

Bruce Lee

370.

Love knows no limit to its endurance, no end to its trust, no fading of its hope; it can outlast anything. Love still stands when all else has fallen.

Blaise Pascal

371.

You know that you are in love when the hardest thing to do is say good-bye.

Mark Overby

372.

There is a sacredness in tears. They are not the mark of weakness, but of power. They speak more eloquently than ten thousand tongues. They are messengers of overwhelming grief...and unspeakable love.

Washington Irving

373

To love is to risk not being loved in return.
To hope is to risk pain. To try is to risk
failure, but risk must be taken because the
greatest hazard in life is to risk nothing.

Ralph W Sockman

374.

May the love hidden deep inside your heart
find the love waiting in your dreams. May
the laughter that you find in your
tomorrow wipe away the pain you find in
your yesterdays.

Anon

375.

I love you, and because I love you, I would
sooner have you hate me for telling you the
truth than adore me for telling you lies.

Pietro Aretino

376.

It hurts to love someone and not be loved
in return, but what is the most painful is to
love someone and never find the courage
to let the person know how you feel.

Anon

377.

Love isn't finding a perfect person. It's
seeing an imperfect person perfectly.

Sam Keen

378.

There is nothing in the world so wonderful as to love and be loved; there is nothing so devastating as love lost.

Sam Keen

379.

To keep your marriage brimming, With love in the loving cup, Whenever you're wrong, admit it; Whenever you're right, shut up.

Ogden Nash

380.

Love, you know, is a funny thing; But the funniest thing about it - Is you never can tell if it is love - Until you start to doubt it.

Anon

381.

To a woman in love, loving too much is not loving enough.

Zelda Fitzgerald

382.

You must love yourself before you love another. By accepting yourself and fully being what you are, your simple presence can make others happy.

Mignon McLaughlin

383.

Sensuality often makes love grow too quickly, so that the root remains weak and is easy to pull out.

Friedrich Nietzsche

384.
It is better to lose your pride with someone you love rather than to lose that someone you love with your useless pride.
Johnny Depp

385.
Love is an untamed force. When we try to control it, it destroys us. When we try to imprison it, it enslaves us. When we try to understand it, it leaves us feeling lost and confused.
Paulo Coelho

386.
He who is in love is wise and is becoming wiser, sees newly every time he looks at the object beloved, drawing from it with his eyes and his mind those virtues it possesses.
Ralph Waldo Emerson

387.
Every man is afraid of something. That's how you know he's in love with you; when he is afraid of losing you.
Sven Goran Eriksson

388.
The way to love anything is to realize that it might be lost.
G. K. Chesterton

389.

This life is yours. Take the power to choose what you want to do and do it well. Take the power to love what you want in life and love it honestly. Take the power to walk in the forest and be a part of nature. Take the power to control your own life. No one else can do it for you. Take the power to make your life happy.

Susan Polis Schutz

390.

To love and win is the best thing. To love and lose, the next best.

William Makepeace Thackeray

391.

Women love us for our defects. If we have enough of them, they will forgive us everything, even our gigantic intellects.

Oscar Wilde

392.

For every beauty there is an eye somewhere to see it. For every truth there is an ear somewhere to hear it. For every love there is a heart somewhere to receive it.

Ivan Panin

393.

The person who risks nothing, does nothing, has nothing, is nothing, and becomes nothing. He may avoid suffering and sorrow, but he simply cannot learn and feel and change and grow and love and live.

Leo F. Buscaglia

394.

Love is a better teacher than duty.

Albert Einstein

395.

Love is an attempt to change a piece of a dream-world into reality.

Henry David Thoreau

396.

Take away love and our earth is a tomb.

Robert Browning

397.

Love the whole world as a mother lovers her only child.

Prince Gautama Siddharta

398.

This is the true measure of love: When we believe that we alone can love, that no one could ever have loved so before us, and that no one will ever love in the same way after us.

Johann Wolfgang von Goethe

399.

God made woman beautiful and foolish;
beautiful, that man might love her; and
foolish, that she might love him.

William Shakespeare

400.

The decision to kiss for the first time is the
most crucial in any love story. It changes
the relationship of two people much more
strongly than even the final surrender;
because this kiss already has within it that
surrender.

Emil Ludwig

401.

It is the same in love as in war; a fortress
that parleys is half taken. *Marguerite de
Valois*

402.

A purpose of human life, no matter who is
controlling it, is to love whoever is around
to be loved.

Kurt Vonnegut

403.

What is love but acceptance of the other,
whatever he is.

Anais Nin

404.

Love is like a fever which comes and goes
quite independently of the will. ... there are
no age limits for love.

Stendhal

405.

Love can change a person the way a parent
can change a baby — awkwardly, and often
with a great deal of mess.

Lemony Snicket

406.

Nothing is mysterious, no human relation.
Except love.

Susan Sontag

407.

Love is kind of like when you see a fog in
the morning, when you wake up before the
sun comes out. It's just a little while, and
then it burns away... Love is a fog that
burns with the first daylight of reality.

Charles Bukowski

408.

Love, n. A temporary insanity curable by
marriage.

Ambrose Bierce

409.

Of all forms of caution, caution in love is
perhaps the most fatal to true happiness.

Bertrand Russell

410.

What is hell? I maintain that it is the suffering of being unable to love.

Fyodor Dostoyevsky

411.

People sometimes say that you must believe in feelings deep inside, otherwise you'd never be confident of things like 'My wife loves me'. But this is a bad argument.

There can be plenty of evidence that somebody loves you. All through the day when you are with somebody who loves you, you see and hear lots of little tidbits of evidence, and they all add up. It isn't purely inside feeling, like the feeling that priests call revelation. There are outside things to back up the inside feeling: looks in the eye, tender notes in the voice, little favors and kindnesses; this is all real evidence.

Richard Dawkins

412.

Anyone who falls in love is searching for the missing pieces of themselves. So anyone who's in love gets sad when they think of their lover. It's like stepping back inside a room you have fond memories of, one you haven't seen in a long time.

Haruki Murakami

413.

The more one judges, the less one loves.

Honore de Balzac

414.

Love itself is what is left over when being
in love has burned away, and this is both
an art and a fortunate accident.

Louis de Bernieres

415.

You can transmute love, ignore it, muddle
it, but you can never pull it out of you. I
know by experience that the poets are
right: love is eternal.

EM Forster

416.

Love is the very difficult understanding
that something other than yourself is real.

Iris Murdoch

417.

It is a curious thought, but it is only when
you see people looking ridiculous that you
realize just how much you love them.

Agatha Christie

418.

I was born when you kissed me. I died
when you left me. I lived a few weeks while
you loved me.

Humphrey Bogarde

419.

Hearts will never be practical until they are
made unbreakable.

Wizard of Oz

420.
Love cannot endure indifference. It needs
to be wanted. Like a lamp, it needs to be fed
out of the oil of another's heart, or its flame
burns low.
Henry Ward Beecher

421.
The person who tries to live alone will not
succeed as a human being. His heart
withers if it does not answer another heart.
His mind shrinks away if he hears only the
echoes of his own thoughts and finds no
other inspiration.
Pearl S. Buck

422.
All love that has not friendship for its base,
is like a mansion built upon the sand.
Ella Wheeler Wilcox

423.
Love is the history of a woman's life; it is an
episode in man's.
Germaine De Stael

424.
The only gift is a portion of thyself.
Ralph Waldo Emerson

425.
Love is the expansion of two natures in
such fashion
that each include the other,
each is enriched by the other.
Felix Adler

426.

Nobody will ever win the battle of the sexes.

There's too much fraternizing with the enemy.

Henry Kissinger

427.

Kindness in words creates confidence.

Kindness in thinking creates profoundness.

Kindness in giving creates love.

Lao Tzu

428.

The heart has reasons that reason does not understand.

Jacques Benigne Bossuel

429.

We can only learn to love by loving.

Iris Murdoch

430.

Absence sharpens love, presence strengthens it.

Thomas Fuller

431.

It is astonishing how little one feels alone when one loves.

John Bulwer

432.

Love looks through a telescope; envy, through a microscope.

Josh Billings

433.

Women may be able to fake orgasms, but
men can fake entire relationships.

Sharon Stone

434.

A kiss is the upper persuasion for
a lower invasion.

Sister Gloria, (Night of Demons 2)

435.

Sometimes I wish I had never met you,
because then I could go to sleep at night
not knowing there was someone like you
out there.

Good Will Hunting.

436.

The love game is never called off on
account of darkness.

Tom Masson

437.

If love is blind, why is lingerie so popular?

Anon

438.

Love is a fruit in season at all times, and
within reach of every hand.

Mother Teresa

439.

Tell me who admires you and loves you,
and I will tell you who you are.

Antoine de Saint-Exupéry

440.

Paradise is always where love dwells.

Johann Paul Friedrich Richter

441.

Thou art to me a delicious torment.

Ralph Waldo Emerson

442.

Love thy neighbor—and if he happens to be tall, debonair, and devastating, it will be that much easier.

Mae West

443.

To love someone deeply gives you strength. Being loved by someone deeply gives you courage.

LaoTzu

444.

Love is a canvas furnished by Nature and embroidered by imagination.

Voltaire

445.

There are only four questions of value in life. What is sacred? Of what is the spirit made? What is worth living for, and what is worth dying for? The answer to each is the same: only love.

Don Juan DeMarco

446.

Don't cry because it's over; smile because it happened.

Dr. Seuss

447.

The heart has no wrinkles.

Marie de Rabutin-Chantal (Marquise de Sévigné)

448.

Falling in love is like jumping off a really tall building. Your brain tells you it is not a good idea, but your heart tells you, you can fly.

Anon

449.

If you have love, you don't need to have anything else. If you don't have it, it doesn't matter much what else you have.

James M Barrie

450.

Love is friendship set to music.

Jackson Pollock

451.

A hug is like a boomerang: you get it back right away.

Bil Keane

452.

Forgiveness is the final form of love.

Reinhold Niebuhr

453.
Love comes with hunger.
Diogenes

454.
When I saw you, I was afraid to meet you.
When I met you, I was afraid to kiss you.
When I kissed you, I was afraid to love you.
Now that I love you, I am afraid to lose you.
Anon

455.
Love is the word used to label the sexual
excitement of the young, the habituation of
the middle-aged, and the mutual
dependence of the old.
John Ciardi

456.
One's first love is always perfect until one
meets one's second love.
Elizabeth Aston

457.
There is hardly any activity, any
enterprise, which is started out with such
tremendous hopes and expectations, and
yet which fails so regularly, as love.
Erich Fromm

458.

Do you want me to tell you something really subversive? Love is everything it's cracked up to be. That's why people are so cynical about it... It really is worth fighting for, being brave for, risking everything for. And the trouble is, if you don't risk anything, you risk even more.

Erica Jong

459.

We are not the same person this year as last; nor are those we love. It is a happy chance if we, changing, continue to love a changed person.

W. Somerset Maugham

460.

Romantic love is an illusion. Most of us discover this truth at the end of a love affair or else when the sweet emotions of love lead us into marriage and then turn down their flames.

Thomas Moore

461.

When one is in love, one always begins by deceiving one's self, and one always ends by deceiving others. That is what the world calls a romance.

Oscar Wilde

462.

Love in action is a harsh and dreadful thing compared with love in dreams.

Fyodor Dostoyevsky

463.

Love is an emotion that is based on an opinion of women that is impossible for those who have had any experience with them.

H. L. Mencken

464.

I never stopped loving you I just stopped showing it

Anon

465.

Love loves to love love.

James Joyce

466.

Love is the hardest habit to break, and the most difficult to satisfy.

Drew Barrymore

467.

Love involves a peculiar unfathomable combination of understanding and misunderstanding.

Diane Arbus

468.

Love without reason lasts the longest.

Anon

469.

If love is the answer, could you please rephrase the question?

Lily Tomlin

470.

I am good, but not an angel. I do sin, but I am not the devil. I am just a small girl in a big world trying to find someone to love.

Marilyn Monroe

471.

There is nothing better for the spirit or the body than a love affair. It elevates the thoughts and flattens the stomach.

Barbara Hower

472.

By all means marry. If you get a good wife, you'll be happy. If you get a bad one, you'll become a philosopher.

Socrates

473.

Romance is the icing, but love is the cake.

Anon

474.

Love is a sweet dream and marriage is the alarm clock.

Jewish Proverb

475.

Love is the same as like, except you feel sexier.

Judith Viorst

476.
True love comes quietly, without banners or flashing lights. If you hear bells, get your ears checked.
Erich Segal

477.
Love is like linen, often changed, the sweeter.
Phineas Fletcher

478.
Love is blind and marriage is a real eye-opener.
Anonymous

479.
Love is the answer, but while you're waiting for the answer, sex raises some pretty good questions.
Woody Allen

480.
The proof of true love is to be unsparing in criticism.
Moliere

481.
It is not so much true that the world loves a lover as that the lover loves all the world.
Ruth Rendell

482.
Affection cannot be created; it can only be liberated.
Bertrand Russell

483.

These two imparadis'd in one another's arms.

John Milton

484.

Love conceals all of one's faults.

Italian Proverb

485.

Saving love doesn't bring any interest.

Mae West

486.

We cannot really love anybody with whom we never laugh.

Agnes Repplier

487.

Love is a lot like a backache, it doesn't show up on X-rays, but you know it's there.

George Burns

488.

Who is wise in love, love most, say least.

Alfred Tennyson

489.

Who ever loved that loved not at first sight?

Christopher Marlowe

490.
We who were loved will never unlive that crippling fever.
Adrienne Rich

491.
Love is too young to know what conscience is.
William Shakespeare

492.
If only one could tell true love from false love as one can tell mushrooms from toadstools.
Katherine Mansfield

493.
I was nauseous and tingly all over. I was either in love or I had smallpox.
Woody Allen

494.
He who is not impatient is not in love.
Italian proverb

495.
We cease loving ourselves if no one loves us.
Anne Louise Germaine de Staël

496.
Work like you don't need the money. Love like you've never been hurt. Dance like nobody's watching.
Satchel Paige

497.

Follow love and it will flee, flee love and it will follow.

John Gay

498.

The hottest love has the coldest end.

Socrates

499.

It has ever been since time began, and ever will be, till time lose breath, that love is a mood --no more --to man, and love to a woman is life or death.

Ella Wheeler Wilcox

500.

Love is the joy of the good, the wonder of the wise, the amazement of the Gods.

Plato

501.

If grass can grow through cement, love can find you at every time in your life.

Cher

ONE LAST THING...

If you enjoyed this book or found it useful I'd be very grateful if you'd post a short review on Amazon. Your support really does make a difference and I read all the reviews personally so I can get your feedback and make this book even better. If you'd like to leave a review then all you need to do is click the review link on this book's page on Amazon.
Other books by the author

The Big Book of Quotes

The Book of Best Sports Quotes

Many thanks for your support